History of Gypsies

History of Gypsies

Venus Sirchie

To order additional copies of this book, contact:
Xlibris
844-714-8691
www.Xlibris.com
Orders@Xlibris.com
819732

Contents

Contents

History

From The Beginning Gypsies Wandering The World Today. More accurate figures re impossible because they are forever on the move and rarely included in a census. They are true nomads that is they travel from place to place never Wanting to settle down never wanting to join an established stable community. They have their own customs and traditions many of which have been manipulate by the non-Gypsy among whom they have traveled but what makes them unique and what they all have in common is their nomadism. They live always temporarily at the edge of cities at the edge of our society. They are for the most part hated and feared. All too often blamed for crimes of which they are not guilty such as kidnapping babies sorcery and in the past even cannibalism they have often been officially discriminated against and Have been almost always been cut by non-Gypsy society of which they themselves ironically want no part they are outsiders and most of them want to remain so they have in some way created and maintained the alternative society that so many people seek and they are proud of it.

There are many different tribes of Gypsies Scholars differ among themselves as to the various classifications there are the word Kalderash Romani Language in Europe the roots of Rom are the same each tribe might have developed different habits and customs but all Gypsies have common on their own way of living. The Rom Gypsies are the same but there are Ramachill Gypsies, Polish Gypsies Task Complicated by The Gypsies themselves. Most Gypsies are illiterate and therefore have no written history in addition they have no sense of the past and are not interested in recounting or even knowing about and if they did these extraordinarily secretive people would reveal nothing to the Gaje as they call the Americans whom they dislike and mistrust and with whom they rarely have any real contact.

Their traditions and customs and ceremonies and even their true names are only reluctantly disclosed to Americans and even then there are reasons to doubt their accuracy it has been said that if you ask twenty Gypsies the same question you will get twenty different answers and that if you put the same question in to one Gypsy twenty times you will also get twenty different answers. There have been occasional accounts of Gypsy life by non-Gypsy who have been permitted to live and travel with the Gypsies but there have been far too few of these. What are Gypsies then for many people juts the word Gypsy conjures up the picture of dirty woman in long skirts apparently sickly babies in their arms begging for money or asking to read palms. For others they are petty swindlers who rent storefronts and deceive a gullible public according to the game their Gypsies must be lazy because they don't work. They find them dark and ugly so they assume they don't wash. They say they are drink far too much and are out of control after a few drinks Gypsies are accused of being sexually promiscuous and their woman are ready to seduce American man which they are always on the lookout for innocent Americans woman. They are said to possess evil powers of magic and to be capable of casting malevolent spells.

Above all Gypsies are charged with cheating and stealing from the Gaje whenever possible they are according to these people a diseased element extraneous to our society. There is however another and equally one sided picture of the Gypsy and this is a romantic one according to this point of view they are a beautiful colorfully dressed people proud and independent gay and life loving and passionate they are carefree and enjoy the simple pleasures of life the sun the moon and the stars these nature lovers too have created a music and dance that throb with passion and joy the woman in their colorful long skirts are irresistible seductive and exciting the dark faced high cheekbones man so proud of bearing are symbols of wild uninhibited powerful these notions have for centuries been encouraged by romantic writers and painters all over the world and they are as untrusted as those others that show the Gypsies to be a totally immoral and disrespectful people.

This book is an attempt to balance these two opposing points of view by giving an honest account of the Gypsy way of life in learning of are origin history and traditions are custom occupations and the changes that modern living has brought about it is possible to reach at least a partial understanding of this greatly misunderstood group that Gypsies originally came from India. This simple fact was unknown until the nineteenth century several hundred years after their first appearance in Europe. Europeans must have wondered where these strangers who infiltrated their mainland came from but not enough to investigate the matter careful in fact the people among whom they traveled showed a surprising lack of curiosity about their origins satisfying themselves with a number of languages basically unconvincing story to explain the roots of these wandering people they called Gypsies perhaps they didn't feel the Gypsies were worthy of scientific investigation perhaps too Europeans prefer to attribute a mysterious romantic past to these bands of wanderers as for the Gypsies themselves they were of little help will for the Gypsies they did not want Sciences to investigate on them the truth before B.C.

An older Gypsies woman pronounced a spell on them to protect her generation it was for no-one to know what Gypsies really mean no one will ever know but the woman who started the curse on the Gypsies they were truly indifferent to their own past and it better suited their purposes to encourage fanciful imaginative explanations of their origins if they said these origins were biblical and therefore Christian and many proclaimed this in spite of the fact that they practiced magic read palms and committed numerous petty thefts they could more easily gain the sympathy of the people and the officials of the towns and cities they visited if instead these roots were tinged with mystery this would enhance their qualifications for fortune telling their most common way of making a living and give them a certain evil power oven the natives many of the Christians of biblical origin were very popular.

According to some the Gypsies were descended from Abraham and Sarah which is all nation descended from Abraham and Sarah. Their endless wandering some people believed it was their punishment for being among those who refused help to Joseph and Mary will it's true after all this is when the Gypsy woman who try to protect her tribe, her name was Fatima Bimbo and to explain they are not working for a living since they were a result of Adam's first marriage prior to the one with Eve they were not concerned with original sin and therefore did not have to earn their bread as decreed by the bible.

Many biblical citations too were used to explained the difficulties of the Gypsies their nomadism is explained by Ezekiel I shall scatter the Egyptians among the nations and in the Book of Genesis a fugitives and a vagabond yourself shalt be in the earth there are other citations from Genesis father of such as dwell in tents predicts their way of living and father of all such as handle the harp and organ could account for their interest in music one of the most widespread legends concerning the Gypsies need to wander was based on the story of the crucifixion of the son of god and the massage came across from a Gypsy man that was known for his dreams and he shared the dream that god village to him that it's ok for the Gypsies to take. When the son of God was being crucified a Gypsy took the nail that the Romans were going to strike the son of god in the heart so from that moment the rumor when around to all the Gypsies so they begin to have the Reputation to steeler.

Gypsies need to wander was based on the story of the crucifixion it seems from this legend that many people were asked to forge the nails of the cross but all refused when they heard the purpose for which the nails were to be used finally some Gypsy smiths agreed to make them and because of this Gypsies were romantic version stated that they were the survivors Minnie Gypsies were known for their metalworkers the ones who live in the French scholar they are the Gypsies that lived in French in but for the ones who escaped through the census with their Christian Waze Gypsies made a way to survive so there was another action about the Gypsies they had no land they agreed that they were foreigners and nomads here on earth obviously people who say such things looking forward to country to call their own if long for the country they came from they would've gone back but they were looking for a better place a heavily home but by faith and they look out for each other so Gypsies were not from India people investigate and by their investigation and knowing people from India and their language hearing the way Gypsies were sounding the same language but the Gypsies picked up a few words so that was why people believe that Gypsies were from India. Gypsies are not from India the investigate thought the Gypsies were just passing through India Gypsies had no solid land they arrived in Europe 1,500 years ago but ever since then Gypsies never explained to whoever they had to they just went along with it. Gypsies they thought that if people think that they are from India they are safe Gypsies were mistake of being India so like it was said Gypsies around the world and for the ones that was in Germany 1939.

The gypsies were slaves for Hitler so the year of 1939 gypsies were suffering bye year of 1945. Hitler decided to have all the Gypsies kill and the Jews he kill 500;000 before he had killed he told his troops if you see any Gypsies man or woman that has gold teeth pulled their teeth out so they did and he around all the gypsies and they were all killed with gas, so for the gypsies never to trust anyone who is not a Gypsy so Gypsies manage to survive no matter what but and the time when Hitler killed some of the Gypsies escape by boat and they were split apart it was families and to find each other after 30 to years later they reunited they were children spread apart how sad.

In the springtime with the advent of warmer weather the Gypsies return to the road awakened and renewed spring is the time for large gatherings and festivals for horse fairs and for pilgrimages to such places as saints Maries De La Mer in the south of for Padua in Italy or Appleby in England which these large and colorful assemblies of Gypsies are an annual opportunity to meet friends and relatives and to exchange news and information once they end each group takes off again to begin its travels usually following the same routes taken the previous year in the past Gypsies have traveled in caravans putting their tents and their few personal possessions into colorfully painted horse drawn wagons and carts in modern times the wooden wagons have been replaced by mechanized means large cars trailers and campers the choice of a campsite winter or summer has always been dictated by several factors proximity to grazing lands was once of great importance as was nearness to a running stream or other sources of water it has been important to find a location where the earth was solid so that their vehicles would not sink into the ground it has always been best to encamp in an isolated area as far as possible from public view.

The Gypsies want their privacy and do not like being observed by local residents also if they are remote from main roads there is less risk of being chased away by local authorities an out of the way site could also prevent their being caught and punished for misdeeds committed in their previous stopping place given these extremely harsh conditions at the mercy of hostile people and unpredictable weather conditions that it can only be wondered how the Gypsies have managed to survive the answer lies not only in their remarkable toughness and will power but also in their tightly controlled social organization which stresses strong family and community ties and in their strict code of traditional laws to a non gypsies their wandering existence might seem aimless and their nomadism might well have been an insurmountable barrier to a regulated life but the Gypsies within their own framework have proven to be a remarkably well organized people the gypsy community that travels together is known as for the Gypsies they were not allow to stay in anyone's countries. They were accused of the woman being which and the man where not allowed to manage horses or sheep unless they would follow their rules and gypsies try to respect but they knew that they will not want to settle down the queen of Hungary it was the year of 1771 realizing that the Gypsies were afraid to stay in the country decided to turn these Gypsies into what she called new Hungarians. They were generously given tools and seed and animals and were to be transformed into farmers in spite of the fact that they had never shown any interest in the land their language was outlawed and they were no longer permitted to trade horses or to sleep in tents the queen's son and successor carried on and do his mother's policy nomadic communities were forced to settle children were required to attend school and go to church and adolescent Gypsies were taken from their families and made to learn trades even Gypsy music could not be played except on special holidays all these measures failed and by the nineteenth century. The Gypsies had gained a certain amount of freedom to be Gypsies by the end of the eighteenth century Spain to realize that expulsion or repression was not the answer to the Gypsies problem it seemed wiser to encourage these people to give up their way of life and to become integrated with the Spanish people. A law was passed that called Rules for Repressing which means depression mini Gypsies were stuffing with anxiety they were chastise vagrant mode of life and other excesses of those who are called Gypsies the way of life was to be repression and not the people Gypsies could follow any career of their choosing any profession that was open Spaniards but only if they renounced their own way of life the same was true in France when the French realized that the Gypsies were stubborn determined to remain in their country laws were enact that encourage the Gypsies to find jobs and settle and giving up their traditions so the Roma Remain on the road they could change their way of living and to be forced to do things that were not allowed in their culture.

The Gypsies Today

The Gypsies Today feel that they are contaminated by the world of the non Gypsy by the factory smoke the polluted air and the poisoned rivers. They yearn to return to the open road their true home What they ask for are permanent camps for the old a large number of conveniently located sites for short stops and adequately equipped and reasonably priced campsites where they might spend the cold winters They ask to for education they might cape with the law and understand and make use of Britain's social welfare system and its benefits. Because of the vastness of the country and the fact that it is composed of so many foreign minorities the Gypsies are less visible in the United States than elsewhere. Most Americans are totally unaware of their presence and according to census and immigration figures they do not even exist Nonetheless large numbers go Gypsies began arriving in the latter part of the nineteenth century mostly from eastern Europe and Spain via South America and according to most estimates there are approximately two hundred thousand Gypsies in the united states today their problems are somewhat different than they have been in Europe and in some ways the Gypsies have suffered less directly than their European counterparts because they are less noticed by the American people.

Generally the Gypsies of America have had to give up a full time nomadic existence. As in other countries horses were of course replaced by motor vehicles cars large buses trailers and campers and these require large quantities of gas which has proved to costly for most Gypsies free camping sites to are scarce for these reasons most Gypsies while retaining their mobility and keeping open all possibilities for travel have temporarily settled in the poor areas of major cities renting small ground floor apartments whenever possible the man generally work on short term jobs that don't require them to stay in one place for any length of time they have been able to find such jobs since they will accept work that non Gypsies will shun their love for horses has been transferred to love for cars and they are often skilled body repairman or auto mechanics. But they insist on maintaining their independence by refusing work that will tie them to non Gypsy employers never for example taking steady work in a garage but undertaking one job at a time such as the repair of a single car it is the Gypsy woman who in the United States as elsewhere earn most of the money the easiest and most honorable way of doing this is through fortune telling.

As soon as possible after their arrival in a city fortunetellers rent a storefront with a room or two in the back these are usually located in poor business areas of the city though some Gypsies are now setting up practices in some of the more fashionable streets of cites like New York. The back area is for living and it is still likely to look like a traditional Gypsy camp with little furniture and with draperies and rags and rugs hung or strewn about the room a mattress or two on the floor and some kind of portable stove or hot plate for cooking the storefront itself is set up as an offish the place of business it is from there that the Gypsies solicit their clients and perform their work some of these ofisas are dark and dingy others are astoundingly luxurious. All contain an aura of mystery the most frequent visitors to Gypsy fortune tellers are middle aged woman who are troubled and problems with which they are unable to cope they turn to fortune tellers not only for soothing predictions but for concrete advice and often they feel that these Gypsy woman are the only ones who will listen to their sad stories if a fortune teller believes that the client is merely curious one fortune teller session at whatever price can be extracted will suffice.

Depending on the client's gullibility and emotional condition the

Gypsy might decide that further sessions are called for at increasingly higher prices if the client is unusually desperate and troubled the ultimate and most profitable of Gypsy confidence games will be attempted the Bajour or Boojoo this word means bag or bag of money and the bag itself is an essential part of this elaborate swindle. Once the fortune teller has learned that her gullible client has money either in a savings bank or hidden in her home she announces that the client's troubles are due to a curse on that money this curse can only be removed by the Gypsy's supernatural powers the money is then dutifully brought to the Gypsy who places it is a bag that is carefully tied and most important substituted by a bag containing worthless scraps of paper the substituted bag is then blessed by the Gypsy who is likely to perform an elaborate ceremony for the occasion the removal of the curse has begun and the mystified client is told to take the bag home and wait for a period of time at least twenty four hours before opening it and removing the newly purified money. As instructed the client later opens the bag only to find not money but worthless pieces of paper.

More humiliated than angry she will usually return to the offisa means office inevitably than it is to late the Gypsy has moved on and is never found. Most victimized woman are to embarrassed to go to the police or even to tell their relatives or friends of the hoax and so few Gypsies are caught and the fortune teller will Usually. Tell her clients that she has to Barry the money in the cemetery so all bad luck will be buried with the money In addition to their talents as fortune tellers Gypsy woman have used their intuitive skills in dealing with social workers and welfare officers they are experts in beating the system in exaggerating their poverty and their needs remaining totally secretive about their real activities this secretiveness characterizes Gypsy existence in America as elsewhere it is maintained for the practical purpose of concealing crime and even more important it strengthens the protective wall that the Gypsies insist on keeping between themselves and the non Gypsies in a consumer society and the United States is a prime example the Gypsies superficially imitate their non Gypsy enemies they buy luxury cars and huge color television sets when possible on credit and without ever paying for them yet they show their contempt for these possessions by battering their cars and letting their expensive television sets fall into disrepair the United States sensitive to the demands of its many ethnic groups and minorities in recent times has not yet faced the problem of its Gypsy population it is a special problem. Other minorities want recognition of their cultures and integration without discrimination into American life. But the Gypsies are suspicious and afraid of being corrupted by non Gypsy societies and do not want to become part of them they fear above all for their children that contact with non Gypsies will lead to the disintegration of their traditionally strong family and community ties and that this will result in juvenile delinquency they fear that their young people will turn to drugs to sexual promiscuity and to large scale crime.

Nonetheless the Gypsies especially the younger ones them activists who see the gains made by other minority groups and want to share in these gains they ask for the respect of the non Gypsy world and for equal job opportunities the first step of course will be education more than ninety five percent of the Gypsies in America are illiterate. However before education is possible Gypsy parents will have to overcome their fear of corruption by non Gypsies and non Gypsies will have to overcome their long hostility toward and misunderstanding of the Gypsies. Many other highly complex problems remain there is the fear that with assimilation many of the Gypsies traditions and customs will disappear that a rich culture will be lost. After all how can a stable society tolerate a group of nomads within its midst without destroying this nomadism. How can Gypsy children always on the move or wanting to be attend regular schools. Nomadism the need to move on remains fundamental to the Gypsy character in fact even those who have settled often paint the ceilings of their rooms blue to remind them of the open sky and these rooms as much as possible resemble Gypsy caves or tents. When spring comes Gypsies all over the world feel an irresistible urge to take to the road even if this means no more then a long spring vacation. Social scientists have only now begun to study seriously the problems of the Gypsies and the possible solutions to these complex problems it is to be hoped that they will turn to the Gypsies themselves a people who have a unique history of adaptability combined with individuality in finding these solutions.

A thorough and sympathetic understanding of these people is certainly a first step in the right direction.

Rules and beliefs of the gypsies and Traditional Occupations

Rules and beliefs of the gypsies and Traditional Occupations are greatly influenced by their nomadic way of life Religion is one example. Most probably because they have not settled among any peoples and have not built stable communities of their own with places in which to worship they cannot be said to have a religion of their own. Though they have for practical purposes adopted the religions of those with whom they have come into contact formal religion has been replaced by faith in magic in omens both good and bad in powerful curses and in miraculous cures.

This body of superstitious some of which are no stranger than the superstitious of non-Gypsies varies among different Gypsy groups but it is to some extent a factor in the lives of all of them Good luck charms amulet's and talismans and talisman Which Means man Made to protect you from evil in if someone is. Meaning you bad its mostly use if someone is meaning you wrong and are community that belongs to the of the non Gypsy is in effect for public use. This explains why when Gypsies steal or beg they feel no guilt for what non Gypsies considered to be immoral acts or punishable crimes Robberies committed by Gypsies and they are traditionally is from Gypsy man who head.

Vision that God said its ok for the tribe steel petty ones have been based on need the Gypsies see nothing wrong in picking grass for their horses stealing wood for their fires or plundering fruits and chickens for their dinners. Robberies are committed not for gain but out of necessity Gypsies point out that they do not rob banks for large amounts of money nor do they steal from each other theft within Gypsy society is a serious crime so they are not natural thieves. Barred from stable occupations by their nomadism as well as by the restrictions of the societies among which they travel petty thievery and begging have seemed to them natural solutions to their problems of day to day living.

Death

Birth, marriage and finally death the three most significant occasions for the Gypsies as they are for most people just as with birth and and marriage these people have the advent of death the burial of the deceased and the post funeral mourning period. Death for the Gypsies is the worst of fates it is a senseless unnatural occurrence which should justifiably anger those who die. Because of this at the approach of death the Gypsy is concerned not only with the pain and heartbreak of the final separation from a loved one but he or she is also profoundly worried about the possible revenge the angry dead might seek against these who remain in the world of the living there are many superstitious portents of death the most common of which is the cry of the ow.l This crying of the owl however means approaching death in many societies and is not unique among the Gypsies.

Obviously a more certain sign of death is serious illness and when the Gypsies feel that one of their group is about to die word is urgently sent to all relatives no matter how far away they might be. As we have learned through fixed contact points the vurma Gypsies are able to find one another in time need even without fixed addresses When an emergency such as approaching death arises relatives and friends can be reached and especially in the case of death all relatives who can possibly do so appear at the bedside of the man or woman who is reaching the end of his life it is necessary to show family solidarity and to obtain forgiveness for dying in the past. There must be no danger of a lingering hidden envy or secret resentment on the part of those who are about to begin a journey to the world of the dead. The dying Gypsy must never be left alone not only out of compassion for his condition but also for fear of possible anger He or she must not die in his or her habitual placed because of this a bed is normally moved in front of the tent or caravan usually under an improvised wall less canopy.

Relatives and friends gather around the dying Gypsy day and night while other Gypsies in the camp take care of practical matters such as feeding the visitors and tracking down those friends or relatives who have been difficult to reach. There are not only tears and lamentations but rage is expressed at the horrors of approaching death. Touching the body of the deceased is discouraged for fear of contamination Because of this he or she is washed and dressed in the finest clothes immediately preceding death if death has been unexpected and this has not been possible a non Gypsy is usually called in to perform these tasks immediately following the death When death finally comes the wailing and moaning increase and from that time until the burial certain traditional customs are observed. Above all there is total absorption in the mourning with no everyday distractions or activities. There is no washing or shaving combing of the hair. No food is prepared. Only the drinking of coffee brandy or other liquors is permitted. Mirrors might be covered and vessels containing water emptied.

An important step to is the gathering together of those things that will be useful to the deceased during the journey from life objects that will be placed in the coffin. These can include almost anything clothing tools eating utensils a watch a pipe a violin things of value such as favored silver or gold ornaments and almost always a small amount of money. Another Matter Gypsies do not cremate there Death. The funeral itself though of little or no religious significance is impressive and moving often a band made up of non Gypsies goes ahead of the coffin playing marches. This band is followed by the widow or widower other mourning relatives and if local religions customs must be followed by a priest. As this procession enters the cemetery the sobbing of the mourners borders on hysteria. The woman might pull their hair or tear their clothes their grief is unrestrained this display of rage and sorrow reaches its peak as the coffin is lowered into the grave. Sometimes the widow will even try throw herself on top of the coffin the mourners generally throw silver and gold coins and bank notes as well as handfuls of earth into the grave the color worn by mourners at Gypsy funerals until recent times when the non Gypsy's black is sometimes adopted has traditionally been white or red White has been thought of as a symbol of purity of protection and of good luck.

Many Gypsy woman will dress entirely in white and the man will wear white ties and gloves and place white bands-around their hats red to has symbolized protection against the evil spirits of the dead and has often been worn at Gypsy funerals. Gypsies feel that the color red brings good luck and are probably drawn to it because of the ancient belief that blood is the source of vitality and life. Red blouses and skirts are common apparel for woman at funerals and man ofter wear red kerchiefs around their their necks red to is a predominantly color in many Gypsy funeral decorations. There is inevitably a large crowd at a Gypsy funeral it is an occasion for friends and family to unite to wish the departed a good journey as he or she enters a new life.

We often read colorful newspaper accounts of the elaborate funerals presumably held for an funeral is the rule and not the exception in Gypsy society and all Gypsies are entitled to enormous funerals. Following the burial the dead man or woman will of course be remembered for the acts he or she performed on earth but all material ties with the dead must be carefully destroyed. Whatever can be burned such as clothing and linens will be turned into ashes articles such as plates cups glasses or jewelry that belonged to the dead will be broken or mutilated. Even animals that belonged to the dead must be killed only the horse is usually excluded from this rule since this obviously imposes great financial hardship on the surviving family it has become more and more usual to sell these objects rather than destroy them but they are sold only to non Gypsies no Gypsy would consider risking contamination by accepting or buying them there should be no trace of the deceased in the Gypsy camp even the use of his or her name is avoided except when absolutely necessary.

Another tradition which follows the funeral is a dinner called a pomana it is an enormous meal usually the first one eaten by the mourners since the death of their friend or relative. Sometimes even the deceased is represented at these meals by another person of the same age as the deceased and dressed in a similar way these pomana are held at various intervals usually nine days six weeks six months and finally one year after the death at each of these. Pomana certain relatives beginning with the most distant ones announce their intention to end their period of mourning. Last to dose after one year are the deceased's immediate family there is no heaven and hell according to the Gypsies life for the dead continues on another level. However there is a great fear among the survivors that the dead might return in some form to haunt the living it is for this reason that the name of the dead should not be mentioned that the body should not be touched and that all objects that belonged to the dead must be destroyed.

The survivors must be protected in every way from the evil contaminating spirits that the dead can emit to avoid this stones or thorn bushes are sometimes placed around the grave. According to the Gypsies the soul of the dead might be reincarnated in another man or animal but most feared of all is the possible reappearance of the dead in the form of a mulo or vampire unless strict precautions are taken this mulo which means living dead might escape from the body and seek revenge on those who had harmed him when living or had caused his dead the mere sight of a mulo who can appear as a vampire or a wolf terrorizes the Gypsy it is a certain sign of bad luck superstition obviously plays a significant role in many aspects of Gypsy life. However of all their rites those connected with death are more filled with fear and superstition than any others there is. Another rule After the funeral A Gypsy will not go to his home on tell they stop somewhere for A few minutes if bad spirits went along with they will leaves them where they stop At and even they will not enter house or Tent.

Marriage

The childhood of a gypsy is an undisciplined one indeed in certain ways Gypsy parents might be called unusually permissive according to non Gypsy standards. That is not to say that the years of growing up are easy ones obviously the rigors and difficulties of the Gypsies nomadic existence serve to toughen the child. However there is little discipline as such. The growing child plays at will improvising entertainments without the aid of special games or toys. There is no organized entertainment. He or she learns whatever skills can be acquired from the mother or Father first by imitating them and finally by helping out his parents whenever possible.

He or she learns the ways of the Gypsies too by observation and at a certain point participation however not complete until the time of marriage. Engagements and marriages are the greatest events the most joyous times in the life of a Gypsy they are the most happily and uninhibitedly celebrated of all periods. Bachelorhood is held in contempt as an unnatural condition while marriage is an essential basic fact of life. Until he is married and most Gypsies marry while in their teens even if he is fifty years old a male Gypsy cannot be called a Rom. There are few rules regarding marriage except that a Gypsy is discouraged if not forbidden from marrying a non Gypsy He or she is also expected to marry someone within the particular tribe. This is a way of maintaining racial purity and individuality. There are exceptional cases in which a Gypsy might take a non Gypsy bride but the latter is expected to renounce her former way of life However this is a rarity and most Gypsies conform by marrying within their group.

The first step in contemplating marriage is the selection of the bride and this all important move varies from group to group in many parts of the world this is done just as it would be done in non Gypsy society. The boy does the courting and when the young couple agree to marry they become engaged and exchange modest gifts parents are consulted but the decision is made by the young people in many other parts of the world however it is the parents and not the young people who arrange the marriage. The prospective bride and groom might be consulted but they don't really count.

According to these groups it is an essential and important duty of the parents to find a bride suitable for their son. They carefully consider all the young unmarried woman in the group evaluating their individual qualities. Looks are of the least importance and the prospective brides are judged on their health stamina strength on their dispositions manners their attitudes toward children and their skills if they can cookie they are adept at telling fortunes if they can maintain a proper home. The character of the girl's family as will as its prestige in the community is also taken into account in these cases no courtship is involved and it is possible that the prospective couple will hardly know each other though there most probably would have been some contact in the encampment. They will usually send a third uninvolved person to sound out the girl's parents on the acceptability of the young man. Rejection of a formal proposal is considered a disgrace and is not to be risked if all goes well the father of the boy then calls on the father of the girl it is a polite and rather serious meeting the purpose being not only to obtain the formal consent of the girl's father but to establish a price to be paid for the bride. This money to be exchanged should be thought of not as purchase of a bride but rather in terms of compensation to the Father for the loss of his daughter. The discussion can be a long one centering on the estimated value of the future bride.

All the would be bride's desired qualities are taken into consideration in addition the girl's father calculates how much his daughter has cost him since birth. After all since she will live and work with her husband's family he is in effect giving her away and his money and training have helped make her what she is. At these meetings there might well be violent disagreements. Sometimes it is necessary to call unfriends as witnesses to the bride's good qualities to argue for a higher price on her behalf or to call in other friends to arbitrate. When an agreement is reached and the price is accepted the meeting ends with the father of the bride to be drinking a symbolic glass of wine. This means that the boy has been formally approved as a husband for his daughter under the stipulated conditions. This arrangement has throughout the years become somewhat less common. Because of greater knowledge of non Gypsy societies many young couples have rebelled against these arranged marriages and against any kind of engagement and have eloped Elopement consists simply of leaving the camp together for a period time.

When they return they are chastised some must pay a nominal fine but eventually they are accepted a married couple. Most young Gypsies however do not elope and for them there is a long period of lively celebration. Following the formal agreement of terms there is often a huge banquet complete with singing and dancing. The bride to be and her family often feign great exaggerated sorrow at having to leave each other. The groom 's family on the other hand pretend to be angry that they are paying such a high price for the bride in the end they decide that the price is will worth it for a bride who will clearly be such a good wife to their son. Frequently a few days after the agreement has been made a ceremony called a plotchka or pliashka will be held. This event is attended by both friends and relatives of the couple.

The symbol of this joyous celebration is a bottle of wine or brandy wrapped in a brightly colored silk handler chief brought to the ceremony by the young man 's father. A necklace of gold coins is attached to the father pretends to look for something he has lost. He anxiously circles the room finally he spots the girl and points a finger at her He then takes the necklace of coins puts it around her neck and warmly embraces his future daughter in law. The necklace makes it clear to all that the girl is now engaged and not available as a bride to any other man Her father in law to be drinks from the bottle and passes it around to the guests When the bottle is emptied it is refilled for use at the wedding celebration. The wedding itself is largely a symbolic act with no religious significance. Though Gypsies usually have had to conform to local laws and customs in the countries in which they marry the non gypsy religious or civil ceremonies have little or no meaning for them. The mere fact that two people have agreed to live together and share their lives together constitutes marriage and no formal ritual is required. This does not mean that they don't take marriage seriously but rather that they do not believe in the importance of a formal wedding ceremony under the jurisdiction of a church or a state.

Nonetheless there are traditional but simple wedding ceremonies performed by some groups of Gypsies in some marriages the bride and groom will join hands in front of the chief of a tribe or an elder of that tribe and promise to be true to each other. A few Gypsy wedding rites are centered around bread In one the bride and groom each take a piece of bread and place a drop of their blood on the bread. They then exchange and eat each other's bread. In another ritual the young couple sit down surrounded by relatives and friends. A small amount of salt and bread is then placed on the knees of the bride the groom takes some of the bread puts salt on it and eats it the bride does the same. The surrounding well wishers then toast the couple asking that they might live together in harmony as do salt and bread The informal joyous festivities celebrating the marriage can go on for several days until guests are weary.

No expense is spared and fortunes borrowed stolen or saved are spent on these happy occasions. Excess is the rule and moderation the exception as the Gypsies enjoy themselves with an abandon they can seldom afford. A huge feast is served and that in itself is an extraordinary event in the life of these people who generally live so frugally. There is usually an open fire over which whole pigs sides of beef and chicken goose are roasted if it is available hedgehog will be served. There might be huge platters of fried potatoes and boiled cabbage stuffed with rice and chopped meat and flavored with herbs and garlic. Drink to is served as generously as is food wine whiskey and beer flow endlessly for this banquet. Violinists play happy rhythmic tunes there are songs and dressed in their finest clothes and they enjoy themselves as they rarely do When the celebration ends and the crowd is ready to leave the gaily colored tent where the festivities have been held it is time for the groom to take his bride to his home. The bride's family kisses the girl and they weep as they unbraid her hair a symbol for her new marital status. Before the groom can take home however there might be an amusing game of the feigned abduction of the bride whose unmarried friends link arms and form a wall so that the groom might abduct his bride. There is much playacting a great deal of screaming and crying on the part of the bride's protectors but the groom happily always wins proudly leading his new bride to his family home which will be their home.

The following morning it is very important that there be some sort of proof of the bride 's virginity either a blood stained handkerchief or a blood stained sheet is displayed as evidence in some cases however an examination by some of the older woman of the tribe is conducted for this purpose. After the wedding. Whatever the proof when it has been established her new mother in law helps the bride knot her kerchief a sign that she is a married woman. She is never again without this kerchief in public but if the bride and if there happens to be none blood found she must be returned to her parents and it will not be hidden she will have a mark on her that no one to pay the price that was pay on her first marriage and her parents. Must return the money back this will only happen if she is not virginal and the parents will try to find out how and who is Responsible so they could pay a fine and punish them but they will never find out her punish is to cut her hair but it hardly happens in the Gypsy community so the celebrations ended a new life begins for the couple who now take their places as full members of the community.

The major change for the man is that he is now socially accepted by other married man and his social life revolves around them and not around his bachelor friends. Changes for the woman are more radical for it is she who leaves her family gathers her eiderdown quilt and her personal belongings and moves in with her husband's family she is guided by her new mother in law and expected to take an active role in the household. Not until the birth of their first child or sometimes not until the birth of several children will the couple move into their own tent or trailer not until they are parents to will they be able to refer to each other as husband and wife before that they use only their first names with each other or in speaking about each other.

Marriages among Gypsies are serious commitments and there are strict obligations on both sides if a girl is found guilty of adultery she must be taken back by her parents who in addition must return the bridal price to the husband's father or if the girl's Father feels she has been mistreated by her husband or in laws he has the right to take her away in many cases these complaints are heard before the kris before a final settlement is made.

Laws and Customs

Birth from the moment of birth the gypsy is subject to the laws and customs developed over centuries and embodied by the kris.

While the Severity of many traditional laws has lessened with time traces of them still remain though they vary from tribe to tribe and from country to country Gypsy life has been a life of hardship of constant exposure to cold winters and hot summers of an endless wandering from place to place. For these reasons severity has been essential for survival and special rites are observed at the times of birth marriage and death. Strict rules come into effect before the actual birth of the child at the time of pregnancy. Most of these rules are based on the belief that a woman is marime impure during pregnancy and for a period of time after the birth of the infant. As soon as a woman is certain that she is pregnant she tells her husband and other woman of the community it is a proud moment and the pregnancy signals a decided change in her status among the group. The prospect of a newborn child is a cause for much joy. Gypsies take great pride in having large families to carry on their traditions. However pregnancy also means that the woman is impure and must be isolated as much as possible from the community and her husband can spend only short periods of time with her during the pregnancy though she continues to live at home it is frequently his job too to take over the domestic duties when she is unable to handle them the birth itself cannot take place in the family's usual home whether it be a tent or a trailer because it would then become impure and have to be destroyed. Because of this woman have given birth in fields in haylofts or in tents specially built for use during delivery and then destroyed in spite of their contempt for non-Gypsy ways an increasing number of Gypsy woman have preferred to leave encamps and give birth in a hospital not because they think they will receive better care but because in that way they will not soil their own homes if the delivery of the infant is to take place outside a hospital only specially appointed midwives or possibly other woman who have experienced maternity are allowed to assist.

There are any number of magic rites that might precede the actual birth the most common of which involves the untying of certain knots so that the umbilical cord will not be knotted sometime all the knots on clothing will undone or cut other times the mother to be's hair will be loosened if it has been pinned or tied with a ribbon. Several rituals to have traditionally followed the birth of the infant. A most frequently practiced one is the purification of the child washing it in running water an act that is separate from any subsequent baptism. After washing is separate from any subsequent baptism. After washing the child might be massaged with oil in order to strengthen it in some cases amulets or talismans are used to protect it from evil spirits. Other symbolic rituals involve the formal recognition of the infant by its father in some cases the child is wrapped in swaddling on which a few drops of paternal blood are placed in other cases the child is covered by a piece of clothing that belongs to the father and in some tribes it is traditional for the mother to put the infant on the ground from which it is picked up by the father who places a red string around its neck thereby acknowledging that the child is his Childbirth itself does not end the state of the mother's impurity it continues until the time of the infant's baptism. This baptism takes place any time from a few weeks to a few months after birth most commonly between two and three weeks.

During this interim period the mother and child are both isolated from the community the mother cannot be seen by any man except in some tribes by the husband. The husband to faces restrictions since he will often be forbidden from going out between sunset and sunrise to keep away evil spirits which might attack the infant during the night.

Theses evil spirits might attack the new mother to but only other woman and never her husband or other man are allowed to protect her because of her impure condition. A new mother is allowed to touch only essential objects and in some cases not cases not even those during what amounts to a period of quarantine. The objects she does touch such as cooking and eating utensils or sheets become impure and must be destroyed.

Though all this generally ends with the baby's baptism certain groups are unusually cautious. For these groups it is two or three months before the new mother will be able to approach her husband or perfume household duties without the of gloves. The newborn child is also considered impure until he or she is baptized Before that its name cannot be pronounced it cannot be photographed and sometimes the baby's face is not even permitted to be shown in public. This period does not end until the baptism when the impurities are washed away by immersion in running water. After that purification the infant formally becomes a human being and can than be called by a name this name however is only one of three that the child will carry through his or her life the first name given remains forever a secret it is generally whispered by the mother the only one who knows it at the time of birth and is never used. The purpose of this secret name is to confuse the demons by keeping the real identity of the child from them the second name is a Gypsy name the one used only among the Gypsies themselves it is conferred informally and only among Gypsies prevalent the real names are given at the baptism and the baptisms is Done only buy A Gypsy couple there are two reasons that Gypsies are Frightened for The Children to the customs of the dominant religion of the country in which the child happens to be born it has little importance for the Gypsies and is merely a practice necessity to be used for dealing with non Gypsies.

Dishes

Gypsies have special rules for washing dishes. And woman Gypsies has special rules of washing dishes it's for separate pails are important not to uses in same water of unclean water win cleaning house or trailer there must have to different washcloth and to different pails one is used for kitchen use and the other is use bathroom and wash cloth is the one that Gypsies woman will never let no one touch her dishes cloth and Gypsies do not allow shoes on eating areas or any close on tables specially underwear were Gypsies eat and a another rule they do not wash there mop in the kitchen sink or in the pail Gypsies will wash there face towel and table cloth only in the pail that is For the kitchen and kept the Eating area spotless.

The Rules is to Bring nothing that is uncle to the Table only Food Marriage woman cannot Washers her Laundry with her Father-in-laws Clothing Together its for Respectable but the Husband and wife its ok. Another Rule For The Marriage woman she cannot go in the Bathroom if There is Annie Gypsy man are Present And Always someone Must be guarding the door just in case A guess might visit And if someone Does stop by the other person will Guard Her only if she a young bride. A Special Rule Woman cannot where pants shorts A woman cannot go swimming if there are man present if A man is on the phone and the phone Has·cord and if its in the way the woman cannot Go over the cord it Means Unhygienic for Gypsies they protect Their Luck the Tradition Bing clean and the woman cannot pass in front of A man in the House Even Between to man she Must go around them in order to Avoid Embarrassment and her Husband will not to have A Argument Between the to of them and if the woman is not Wearing Long skirts she Must cover her Legs with A Blanket or coat when sitting when her Husband is invited to some one House and if she wearing Short Skirt Her Husband will Be Question why Did he Allow Her to Dress Unappreciated And to Make sure it won't Happen Again. And The clothes that she was wearing will Be Destroyed so she will never where them Again so the clothes will Be Burned And it could Bring sin on Her And on Her Husband and the Elder will she is Evil and if in would Happen she must go to the Elder And Ask them to forgive her And will never where them again so the clothes will be burned.

Traditional Occupations

Nomadism has influenced every aspect gypsy life and it has been along with their refusal to depend on the and it has been along with their refusal to depend on the non-gypsy for a steady income the determining factor in the kinds of occupations they have chosen Jobs undertaken by members of a stable settled community would be impossible for them and they have traditionally sought work that could be done by a people on the move work that required little and light equipment as well as work that did not call for year round attention. Because of this agriculture which would have necessitated permanent residence had never interested them until recent times when Gypsies began to take on occasional summer jobs as farm workers because they have shown themselves to be remarkably adaptable to changing conditions in different countries it is impossible to do more than generalize about the traditional occupations of the Gypsies. However there have been two conditions that a job must meet before it will beef interest to a Gypsy one is that it must allow the Gypsy to be free to travel and the other is that it should call for as little steady direct contact with the non-gypsy as possible in general Gypsy occupations are divided by sex. Men are the artisans while women offer services such as fortune telling and sell what the man produce it is the woman who bring in the money and the woman who are largely responsible for spending it and giving it to the man when they need it.

Gypsy vendors have always been a common sight near any Gypsy encampment Because their movements and travels are always uncertain they are unable to build up a steady clientele in any one place for this reason they are forced to try to sell their wares to passersby or by going from house to house the articles they sell are of little value minor objects such as baskets brooms rakes wooden spoons and combs because these products are easily obtainable from regular local suppliers and the ones made by Gypsies are often of not very good quality their selling is almost the equivalent of begging there are certainly some good craftsmen among the Gypsies but for the most part people buy from them out of pity or even more frequently merely to get rid of them one area in which male Gypsies have traditionally excelled is that of metalwork they were known as metalworkers from the beginning of their history. But not all gypsies work his metalworkers they were known for their fortune telling Gypsies. There is after all something mysterious about the work of the smith who bends metal to his will with the aid of fire the art of the forge is an ancient one making use of the fundamental elements of water and fire and the Gypsy seems to have learned this extraordinary art while in India where it was considered a disgraceful occupation not worthy of the higher castes the Gypsies have been experts in all forms of metalwork whether it be as tinsmiths coppersmiths or silversmiths they have made nails tools kitchen equipment and arms they have been skilled at plating objects with tin or embossing and engraving pieces of jewelry some have been masters at making false coins and others especially in Hungary and Rumania have been gold washers collecting gold deposits from the bottoms of rivers.

Gypsies have not only been master smiths but they have also shown great ingenuity in devising relatively light equipment such as forges and hammers which are necessary to their work and which can be more easily transported than can the generally massive tools used by smiths just as male Gypsies have always shown an affinity for working with metal they have long been renowned as horse dealers. Because horses were essential for transportation in the early days of migration their care and treatment were of great importance to the Gypsies the Gypsy in addition feels great affection for this animal which has played such an important part in his life no one is more capable of capturing wild horses breeding them and then transforming them into workable animals than the Gypsy the skills of these people in curing the illnesses of horses that others less knowledgeable would discard as hopeless have served them for centuries often they would trade a good horse for an apparently less healthy one collecting needed money for the difference by caring for these sick horses and putting them into good condition they were later able to sell them for a far higher price than the original one paid skilled dealers as well the Gypsies made a specialty of attending horse fairs these were major occasions in their lives occasions for pleasure as well as business they were adept at pointing out the advantages of their own horses which had been carefully taken care of before the fairs and concealing or minimizing their defects by the same token they knew how to emphasize the disadvantages of those horses they were interested in buying thereby bringing down their prices the horse has always been an important economic factor in the life of the Gypsy and the Gypsies understanding of this animal has been widely recognized so much so that for many years it was common among the country people of eastern Europe to bypass the village veterinarian and go to a Gypsy to cure an ailing lovers and next to the horse the animal they have shown greatest interest in is the bear. Because of this Gypsies traditionally have found work as bear leaders that is man who could train bears for entertainment purposes it was not an uncommon sight for many years especially in Europe to see a gypsy leading a dancing bear through the streets and collecting coins from amused passersby even today some of these bear leaders are found in eastern Europe the occupation for which the Gypsy has always been most famous is a woman's activity fortune telling. Indeed the classical and most familiar image of the Gypsy women is that of the fortune teller there are three main reasons that fortune telling has appealed to the Gypsies first of all it gave them an aura of mystery and of magic in this way it served as a means of self-protection building up a fear of curses or spells in the non-Gypsy Quite often to since it was the one means of intimate contact with the non gypsy world fortune tellers were useful in learning of the social political and economy climate of region they might contemplate visiting for a length of time their clients often took them into their confidence revealing facets of local conditions the Gypsies would otherwise be unable to judge finally of course fortune telling was a relatively simple way of earning money from and winning a degree of power over a gullible public Gypsies have been adept at every kind of prediction they have read tea leaves seen visions in crystal balls and analyzed the future from the reading cards.

Above all they have been expert in palmistry judging a person's fate character and aptitudes from the shape of hands and fingers and the designs of lines in the hand though they claim that their great powers of prediction come from heaven the real skill of fortune tellers lies in their great shrewdness in judging human character and in exploiting human weaknesses to please their believing clients they most often predict a favorable future the lonely girl will find a rich and handsome husband the man will find a rich and beautiful bride and they will have a long and happy marriage to strike a degree of fear and awe there will be mysterious warnings of perils which might well be avoided by rather costly preventatives provided of course by the Gypsy the Gypsy fortune teller is a good judge of human nature she knows that most people remember what comes true and forget what does not she knows to that she is capable of adding an exotic exciting element to the life of an insecure non-Gypsy and she feels or pretends to feel that she is doing a service by in some way acting as a confident to these lonely people she is playing on their fears and supernatural but only on those of the non-Gypsy for Gypsies though a superstitious people themselves never practice their skills as fortune tellers on other Gypsies.

Although fortune telling is basically a joke as they would said hoax Gypsy musicians and dancers have made a genuine contribution to the non-Gypsy world Gypsy soloists and orchestras have entertained non-Gypsies since they first came to Europe. Documents show that they were favored as court musicians in Hungary in the fifteenth century and throughout Europe for several centuries since then the instruments preferred by Gypsy musicians have been guitar the lute percussions especially cymbals the cello and the violin the violin has best been able to express a wide range of emotions for the Gypsies though their orchestras have included the clarinet they seldom use brass or wind instruments their music is gay and bright and it can also be moving and soulful since the large majority of Gypsies have been unable to read music their skill at improvisation is all the more remarkable. Apart from their undisputed role as excellent performers their actual contribution to the composition of music has been disputed composers as far apart as Franz Liszt and Bela Bartok have acknowledged the marked Gypsy influence on the colorful rhythmic music of Hungary However it seems clear that what the Gypsies did was borrow from the music of the countries they passed through in their travels adding to it their own flavor rather than creating a wholly new music of their own the same is true of the so called Gypsy music of Spain which has enjoyed enormous popularity when we note the great differences between Spanish Gypsy music and Hungarian Gypsy music it becomes clear that neither is Gypsy music as such but both are brilliant and inventive adaptations of the local music to which the Gypsies have made certain original contributions this is also the case with so called Gypsy dance which is largely the flamenco a dance that originated in Andalusia and which has become famous throughout the world this stirring dance performed by proud men and seductive women stamping their feed and snapping their fingers with awesome intensity and passion is largely associated with the Gypsies some of the finest flamenco dancers have certainly been Gypsies.

Nonetheless switch so much Spanish music what the Gypsies did was to adapt and even popularize a dramatic and exciting dance form that is traditionally Spanish and not Gypsy if occupations are defined as activities by which a people make a living it is at this point that one of the most common and least commendable ways that Gypsies survive economically must be mentioned petty thievery and begging these activities are not to be excused or condoned they are justifiably abhorred by non Gypsy social.

However they should be understood within the context of Gypsy customs and morals as well as the Gypsies possibilities for obtaining their basic necessities Fundamental to Gypsy thought is complete contempt for the non Gypsy for whom they feel no love or affection no real ties at all. Because of this stealing from the Gages not considered a crime it is an achievement a proof of the superior cleverness of the Gypsy so by the same token is begging the Gypsy beggar a women deliberated looks dirty She scratches and coughs and does her best to be repulsive so that the Gaje will give her money just to get rid of her the Gypsies believe that stealing from or begging from the non Gypsy is justifiable for other reasons. First of all since Gypsies have no real sense of private property or possessions outside their own community.

Another Personal Habits

Gypsies A misconception with no basis in fact is that Gypsies are often drunk. Another misconception is that they will eat anything they can get their hands on. While undoubtedly true that their wandering existence and poverty have forced them to eat foods that might be distasteful to other peoples there are very strict taboos against foods chief among them horse meat which is eaten by non-Gypsies in many parts of the world. Any Gypsy eating horse-meat will be severely punished or even banished from the tribe the relationship of the horse to the Gypsy has always been such a close one that it is unthinkable to eat this animal. Cats and dogs are also forbidden as foods. These animals have no special meaning for the Gypsies but they consider them unclean because they lick themselves.

Cleanliness is a very special matter for the Gypsy one that is little understood by outsiders who most often consider. Gypsies a dirty people unconcerned about personal hygiene this misunderstanding is certainly encouraged by the Gypsy who often wants to appear dirty knowing that this is one sure way of avoiding close contact with the Gaje whom he or she really thinks of as dirty. The Gypsy code of hygiene is based on the concept of marime it is a complex and rigid system. An understanding of this fundamental part of Gypsy life will make it clear why the Gypsies feel that the Gaje are unclean this marime is related to the marime concept adopted by the Gypsy courts but while the legal term means rejected the term when applied to personal hygiene means dirty or polluted. Much of it stems from the division of a Gypsy woman's body into two parts above the waist and below the waist. A woman is clean from the waist up and polluted from the waist down. There is no shame connected with the upper part of the body woman are allowed to expose their breasts and they will often use their brassieres as pocketbooks there is nothing wrong with a man reaching into a woman's brassiere to take a few coins. The lower part of the body is however an object of shame because it is associated with menstruation the belief that menstruation is a sign of impurity is not unique among Gypsies and is widespread among many primitive societies the fact that blood flows without injury seems to be for these societies the proof of a bodily impurity located in the lower part of a woman's body many of the traditional laws of hygiene deal water.

For example a Gypsy must wash only in running water. A shower would be acceptable but a bath would not be for the Gypsy would be sitting or lying in dirty stagnant water. Dishes cannot be rinsed in the same sink or basin that is used for washing personal clothing. The kitchen sink like we said before therefor it cannot ever used for washing. Brush your teeth or spit and the kitchen sink for the Gypsies it's to be clean it pure were the place they eat the Moe's in porter place is the kitchen not ever be used for washing one's hands Gypsy tribes have set specific and very rigid rules for the drawing of water from a river or stream the water from the farthest point upstream therefore the purest is used for drinking and cooking. Working their way downstream the water is used in this order washing dishes and bathing washing or nourishing horses washing clothes and at the nearest point downstream washing the clothes of pregnant or menstruations woman on order to make certain that there will be no impurities.

Making a Living

Some sell flows some do Body work and the ones that do something that is not right will go to jail and Some don't And today there are Gypsies That Are working Carnivals 2021. They don't do anything else. And there Are in Every state A Gypsy Pastor each state. There are 3 to 4 who Belong in the same state And are clan was Saved in the year of nineteen eighty six. Pretty much its when 70% of Gypsies were saved there was Pastor that was from California and he was A Russian Gypsy And he cane to Chicago Illinois to preach the word of god And his name was John Zico Gypsies would call him pastor John. John and Another special person that it was A Privilege two know A wonderful person, Mr. Joe Eli he was Gypsy but he was Born with ADHD But joey was A person who had a Lotta off love for anyone he loved to Work He would go and Get Job Doing window.

Shoeshiner and he made Living he was A hustler in the Neighborhood he lived in there was A Restaurant it was Owned by Palestinians And ones A year they would Have Rajab And he Made himself A Connection to At the door and the Customers donate him money. People loved Him we grew up together it was never A dull moment he Made people Laugh And he Worked in church As A Deacon the church he work At Saint mart church for nine years joey was full Gypsy Date of Birth 1957 -year

Death December 2020 it was so sad for us and for all the world will are Tribe his death was from Covid 19.

One More Tradition that i must tell you Gypsies do not believe to own A cat. They Believe that A cat Bad luck if A Gypsy Family would Have A cat they will not Visit they feel that the cat will Put Curse on them very few own cats Even been A Christian they won't Allow it and even A bird they feel that the bird will Take the little ones Life and there is.

One More Thing, A Gypsy will not work for no one they work Self-employed. There's not one Gypsy That's A doctor A lawyer A Gypsy does not work and any office How could they they never went to school But they made living And they Have A good life.

Modern Gypsies

I have been Among the Gypsies since Forty nine Years and its has been A long Journey and A Experience to be with Remarkable people will My Mom Eloped With A Gypsy Man and the year of nineteen seventy two it was the year that My Biological Dad Passed away my Dad was not A Gypsy He was American and my life was changed Right From that very moment there were no more school and there I was Surrounded with people that are Called Gypsies will My mom was Embarrassed that she Married American But She Loved My Father And she choose to Live A Gypsy and Traveling Life and There were about sixty trailers and My step Father had A very big trailers and the Gypsy Rule.

The young couple Starts out width Smaller trailers and when it was dark they would make fire to have light and when it was Morning the woman will start fire to make coffee when there husband's wake up to go to work and all the woman Had Scars on there Head And prepare A meal. The mans work was roofing or Black topping they were Self employed and sometimes the woman when the woman go to Town they Approach Someone they will feel that person will listen to what she head to say and then the woman will know and Feel that's the person to tell their fortune to the Gypsy woman know when it's ok so After A few Days would pass the Gypsies feel that it's Time To Move to the next please and do the same thing when the non Gypsy sees them the police make us to leave their town so Gypsies are always on the alert for there children for not Been in School they were afraid to allow There kids to go to School Because That they would kidnapping or Rape And Gypsies was not to settle down just for A little bit add a time and they would go Right back to the traveling life it was so Hard for the Gypsies the non Gypsy would chase them out where ever they were at so the Gypsies would keep on move to state to state it was the year of nineteen seventy five.

After few years Later the Alders Decided to go to Pensacola Florida and Rent some Apartments and some of the other Gypsies went to a different area and we were about 25 to 30 families and After a few days past it was a night that would never will be forgotten when we were Attack by the KKK. It Started at 3:45 in the Morning we were the only ones in the whole complex and Gypsies are very Scared of Ghost the noises that they were making. The Sounds to wake us up and the wife of the leader of the Gypsies did not fear goes she was the first one to wake up go outside the partisan building we were right around her maybe from 40 to 50 feet and her name was like And she screamed Get up my people we're being attacked by KKK we All got up and Terrified Didn't know what was Going on the only thing we see people Dressed in white and Throwing Arrows of Fire and shouting get out and Burned one of are family members car so the KKK stop. About 5 pm in then they made sure that everyone was out and they made the owner of the car that they Burned to Remove it off the property so one of the Gypsy man push it out what is truck are Trailers were part in an empty space are children were scared for months from their the Gypsies on the road Again they Rented Beautiful camera ground and we celebrated Drinking and dancing Cooking roasting pigs lambs Turkeys the Celebrated when on for two days and been happy that no one got hurt the Owner of the campground loved it he said he never met such remarkable people in his life he stood with them celebrated and the leader of the tribe told him everything And the man from the camp Felt Sorry For us and the Gypsies Did not try to Scam him. Because of his kindness the Gypsies made sure not to leave to Dirt on his camp but one of the man came to the elder and said this man is acting too nice something is not right and then they start thinking so the leader said if anything happens we will be ready this time so they were Saying let's just leave go on the road the leaders name was Larry so Larry call his mom she was a woman who senses Evil.

After that night with kkk she left her daughter and wanted to stay with her son so there were other family members who had their own group. Because the group Larry had were not speaking terms they traveled on one road but Didn't stay together so the mother of Larry if she would've been when kkk were about show up she would've known so then she said there is no harm here so A few days after the Gypsies were on the road again going to Memphis Tennessee will Hopping to see Elvis presents the Gypsy loved Elvis and they made it there business to see him will on the road Again Going to Texas so we Arrive to are Destination and we part are. Trailers in park side so the liter would go head to Find a place to state they did want to show all of us we Heard nowhere to stay we Had 75 to 80 trailers so they thought if the owner sees so many Gypsies it'll be a problem so we waited and we seduce bye News Reports and they were Harassing us and us children Started to chase them Away not one if are Alders want it to Talk what them so they Allowed Us to do what we wanted is to Throw food and toilet paper we were Going to Throw Rocks but if we Did that it be a problem so they left and if we would've Let them interview it would been A Unspeakable words and lies so we did not Appreciate That so whatever we would go non Gypsies would look it Us like we were wild Animals just Because we are Gypsies Dan we stood campground tell we all Renton Houses for A few Months and the way they Manage to Renton without Credit Event without id They New how to Talk there way in they Did and After we Decided to go Back on the Road Again we had some Relatives who were with circus.

The woman were Telling fortune and the Man were Selling food so we did not want to cause them any problems so we kept on traveling from State to State Until the Elders Gathered together And decided to leave the traveling life and settle down it was getting too hard what the law police chases whatever we would go so it was Abigails Decision to Make Because there was no going back on the road so one of the the Gypsy man his name was jimmy Suggested to make A School for

all the Gypsy Kids Jimmy Stvte was Educated man He Made A man
from Sweden and was Willing too Help him to Teach the Children but
they denied it and the Decision they Told Jimmy that they are going
to Settle Down Somewhere Wes and they Appreciate all he have Done
so. A few Months Later we were Still on the road and going and going
and Renting camps that were hunted but I can Lie it was funny So the
Late year of nineteen Seventy nine.

The Gypsies Finally Decided to Sell there Trailers that New That
if they have the Trailers they will Never Stop Traveling so the Final
Decision was made they all Decided to go to Illinois were the joneses the
Mitchell bimbo john's the Eli's Dimitrio Now the Ristick And Stevens
and the Evans And the lee's where never into the travel life their first
generation escaped and there ancestors who made sure there their sons
would never enter the war and to Blend in inn big cities Stupa head
A way Elopes to his generation even the ones who Traveling york city
was the capital But the Stevens Move to lllinis and the lee's it was Early
1900s they live the city life but tell fortune so for Larry John And the
Mitchell and the bimbo the Dmytro's and the Eil's made their decision
the ones that I mansion Earlier and Finally made decisions to move to
lllinis and never to go on the road again so the john's And The Eli's
met up with the costellos frank miller was the leader for the miller's
the one's who was Residence in Illinois there were some Costellos who
live's in Toledo Ohio so for Larry John and His crew we were About
176 Occluding children and Resign And Rental apartments houses And
Blend in And from That day the Gypsies never return to Road it was
hard for ones who never lived in houses But they new it had to end and
for the Mitchell group they went South they and Did the same As the
john's Did the bimbo's Went west the Dimitrios went with the Mitchell
And the Eli's stud with the John's will the Eli's And the john's were
Related And they Study Together just as the john's and the Eli's will
there is A Another Gypsies Rule Gypsies were Always religious it was
the year of late 1979 A Gypsies man who was From Friends heading to
los angeles is name Sam Mitchell he Wanted to Bring the word of god
to all the Gypsies Generations He was the First Gypsy Pastor among
the Gypsies and the Message went all over the Gypsy clean and Gypsies
were getting saved. All because of him And he Ordain the First Gypsy

Pastor in the year of 1984 and A Very blessed man is name was pastor john Zico A lot of Gypsies Changed they're less names if there less name were not in English so pastor john wanted to move to Chicago he felt god wanted him to preach in that city and to Save people and that's exactly what he did Between him and the pastor from Friends they Saved thousands of Gypsies And God Blessed them And A another Rule About Gypsies Used to Believe About there love ones not to purchase life insurance they if they have insurance on that person that they are wishing Death so As time went by more like years As being Christians they Didn't believe in the old Traditions Waze.

A new live for the Gypsies were All Saved and Every state there is a pastor So The old traditions were Stopped i will Say A few things will remain in the Gypsy Waze first thing they will never stop there woman to where gold A few Traditions will end the Bright doesn't need to prove if she virgin when a newborn baby is born the mother Does not need to stay in the room for 30 days the father does not need to put blood on the infant don't need baptized the baby so the biggest rule will never change the kitchen Those are the 5 the rest of the rules remain.